Pony

CAROLYN S. BABER

ILLUSTRATIONS BY LUKE FLEISCHMAN

Richmond Saddlery Press
Richmond, Virginia
Copyright© 1990

To my three children who made it possible.

Second Edition 1994

Isn't that a funny name for a pony? I mean just Pony? Because it is perfectly obvious to anyone that she is a pony. Pony is not the only name she had, nor is it the first name attached to her, but it is the one she learned to like best, and this is the story of how she found her name and home in this exciting world where we all live.

Pony was born on a proper pony farm to very respectable parents. Both her mother and father, and their mothers and fathers, and all her aunts, uncles and cousins were registered American Shetland ponies.

Soon after her birth, her owner sent in an application for her to be entered in the family book of all registered Shetlands. She was officially called Top Hat's Golden Lady with the distinguishing number 97173-A. So you can see how her first name became Top Hat's.

It was a proud day for Top Hat's mother when the certificate was returned with Top Hat's Golden Lady embossed in big black letters. Her owner placed it in the tack room with all the other certificates.

After that, Top Hat's mother was sure that Top Hat's would be bought by someone who would allow her to contribute to her family's impressive list of accomplishments. There were many choices open for her.

She could be a harness racing pony and thunder down the track to the winner's circle.

She could be a hunting pony pounding behind the hounds over hill and valley.

She could be a parade pony and carry a flag as the leader.

She could be a circus pony and perform before hundreds of cheering children.

But none of these dreams came true because she was bought by a kindly man who wanted a pet for his grandson, Andy.

Top Hat's and her mother were humiliated by the prospect of Top Hat's being a pet and not being a racer or hunter or leader in a parade. So, Top Hat's didn't go to her new home happily. She pouted and felt sorry for herself. She let her ears droop and her tail hang low.

Her new surroundings were pleasant enough. The farm had white fences and nice roomy paddocks. Top Hat's had clean straw each day and plenty of hay, but being some child's pet was a burr under her saddle. She just didn't like the idea.

Pretty soon Andy came out for a ride. He was a quiet boy and Top Hat's diligently carried him around the farm. They had some good times together. The only problem was he called her Brownie.

Of course, she was brown, with a long golden mane and tail. But you have to admit, Brownie does not sound as important as Top Hat's Golden Lady. Nevertheless, Brownie became her second name.

So, Brownie, as Andy called her, began spending her time standing in the corner of the paddock thinking about her situation and trying to figure out what she could do to make life a little more exciting. She thought and thought, and the only thing which made any sense to her was to leave the farm at the first opportunity.

She didn't have to wait long for a chance to leave. Someone left the latch loose on the paddock gate, so she carefully squeezed through the gate and trotted off down the lane to see what was on the other side of the farm.

On her first outing, Brownie found an apple orchard. She ate and ate, munching greedily, until she satisfied her appetite for the juicy fruit.

This escape was so much fun that she decided to go back to the apple orchard every time she could. Soon, she even learned to open the latch by herself.

It didn't bother her that these adventures upset Andy. In fact, she was glad to get back at everyone for making her just a pet. Most of all, she resented being called Brownie. She backed her ears each time Andy used that name.

But, all the while Brownie was running away and making life pretty miserable for Andy, something else was happening.

Every day Andy's sister Courtenay was coming out to see her. Courtenay was a little girl and just barely came up to the pony's nose. Courtenay brought Brownie delightful tidbits: carrots, apples, celery. No matter what Courtenay was eating, she would share it with the pony—peanut butter and jelly sandwiches, doughnuts, and once in a while, a box of raisins. They were a real favorite.

Courtenay would sit on the fence and talk to her, or squat on the ground and point her finger in the pony's face and say, "Now, Pony, you must not run away again because I love you, and when you run away, I worry and worry. You are a nice pony, and I love you so much. Please don't run away again."

Well, she didn't pay much attention to Courtenay. After all, she was just a little girl, and besides, she was really irritated at being called Pony. That name was even plainer than Brownie. But she did find herself waiting for Courtenay every day and each time she ran away, she felt more and more sorry for the little girl, when she came back.

Courtenay kept coming to the barn to see Pony every day. She rubbed her nose, petted her, fed her, talked to her, combed her mane and tail, and she never forgot to tell her how much she loved her. "I love you, Pony," she would whisper when she left.

One day Pony got away very early in the morning and because she had already seen all the things close by, she just kept going, farther and farther, until she got to the huge state forest. This was new. She kicked up her heels and galloped through the trees. It was quiet except for the crackling leaves under her hooves. She was having great fun pretending she was a giant stag, king of the forest. On and on she went until it began to grow dark. Then, she realized she was lost.

All night she stayed in the forest, alone. The next morning a blanket of snow had covered everything—her tracks, her coat, and most surely, the snow had covered her spirits. For days she walked and walked looking for a way out of the forest. She thought about the farm and Courtenay and missed them more than she would ever admit, even to herself.

Each morning she thought she would find her way out and each evening she thought she would not live through another long night.

In fact, Pony would probably still be in the forest if it had not been for a friendly hunting dog who happened by and offered to show her the way out.

When Pony saw the farm, she kicked up her heels and trotted up the lane. Courtenay ran to her, choked with tears of relief. "Pony, Pony, I knew you would come back. I knew you would because I love you so much. You won't ever run away again."

And you know, Courtenay was right. Pony has not run away again, and her name is still just plain Pony. She learned what we all must learn. The thing that makes us happiest is to be loved and wanted by someone we love.